Combating Parental Alienation And Its Impact On Children

Info That May Help Preserve Your Relationship With Your Child From An Alienating Parent

Kelly Peterson, Esq.

ISBN: 978-1-941645-06-2

Designed and Published by:
Speakeasy Publications
73-03 Bell Blvd, #10
Oakland Gardens, NY 11364
www.SpeakeasyMarketingInc.com
888-225-8594

DISCLAIMER

This publication is intended to be informational only. No legal advice is being given, and no attorney-client relationship is intended to be created by reading this material. If you are facing legal issues, whether criminal or civil, seek professional legal counsel to get your questions answered.

Law Office of Kelly Peterson
2696 N University Ave.,
Suite 240 Provo, UT 84604
(801) 375-0484
www.kmpetersonlaw.net

Testimonials

"He is an extraordinary attorney, and stands out among the attorneys in this area. In my experience, Mr. Peterson has always been well prepared for any case in which he takes a position. He does his homework, meets with his clients, and is reasonable, as well as smart in his presentations to the court and to opposing counsel. It is a pleasure to work with him because I know he always has a factual and valid legal basis for the claims he makes. He never takes a case personally, but makes decisions based on objective criteria and good research. Further, he is personable and honest."

- Lori Fowlke, Local Attorney with over 20-Year Experience in Family Law

"Kelly has consistently proven himself to be a highly skilled litigator. His pre-trial preparation is among the most thorough that I have ever seen. What perhaps has been the most surprising aspect to me is how efficient his methods are. Time is not wasted, and quality work product is quickly produced. He has earned a reputation in the legal community as a strong, aggressive trial lawyer. Although he is always willing to work collaboratively toward mutually agreed case resolution, he is never afraid of engaging in the full battle, when necessary."

- F. Richards Smith, former director, Office of Guardian ad Litem

"I am impressed by Kelly's work ethic and efficiency. He works extremely hard and is always ultra-prepared for his court hearings and trials. He has refined his system of investigating and case preparation to be extremely efficient and effective. Kelly is respected by the local bar and judges, as being very competent, consistently prepared, exhibiting good judgment, and being a first rate trial lawyer. Kelly is considered to be among the most expert and proactive of district court Guardians ad Litem (GAL) attorneys in Utah. Kelly possesses integrity, honesty, civility, dependability, and professionalism. He has also demonstrated grace under pressure repeatedly. He has performed an outstanding job in a very difficult and high-conflict area of law."

- R. John Moody, Managing Attorney, Fourth District Office of Guardian ad Litem

"Kelly has a unique ability to see to the heart of complex issues, dispense with frivolous matters, and focus on what is important. He has strong analytical ability and argues persuasively. Kelly has an easy, thoughtful manner that makes him...easy to work with. However, when he makes up his mind on the right course of action, he defends that position with firmness and tenacity without being overbearing. Moreover, I have observed Kelly to be both honest and ethical."

- Judge (retired) Norman H. Jackson, Utah Court of Appeals, Previous Employer

"We consider him to have been a valuable asset to this firm. He has good judgment, integrity, and common sense. Further, Kelly is a skilled and capable advocate, both in transactional work and in litigation. He zealously represents his clients, but does so in a civil, professional manner, without the need to resort to posturing, intimidation, or similar tactics. We have also observed Kelly to be thorough, thoughtful, and detailed in all aspects of his practice. The foregoing qualities, together with a solid courtroom presence, have led Kelly to be well-liked and respected by the local bar and judges. Kelly engenders confidence in his clients, who find it easy to trust his judgment and advice. Most importantly, Kelly is dependable. There has not been one occasion where Kelly has failed to accomplish a task by the deadline, and the ability to depend on that trait makes him invaluable in our practice."

- Jeff Ouderkirk & Jeff Hollen, Previous Employers

"Kelly and I have had the privilege of working on many cases together. Through his diligence and dedication, lives were saved. Kelly is a thorough professional. Without question he is dedicated to his perception of the best interests of his clients. Kelly is decisive. He is not afraid to make a decision. I have observed him being confronted by hostile parties. In such circumstances I have always observed him to be calm, poised, and reflective. Kelly Peterson will continue to be a credit to the legal profession."

- Brent Young, Local Attorney with over 33-Year Experience in Family Law

"He is passionate in his representation of the children in his care. Kelly is thorough in his trial preparation. I do not believe there is an attorney in Fourth District who understands the Rules of Civil Procedure and Rules of Evidence better than Kelly. He spends the time to meet with his clients, parents and others to be able to make recommendations as to the best interests of the children. He is both determined and persistent in advocating for them. I know there are children who are alive and healthy today because of Kelly's willingness to go the extra mile. He will take a stand, and follow through with the steps necessary to get to a positive outcome. I have also seen Kelly serve as a very effective partner in mediations. He works with the parents in a thoughtful and kind manner. Kelly will be a wonderful asset."

- Sandra Dredge, Local Attorney with over 21-Year Experience in Family Law

TABLE OF CONTENTS

AUTHOR INTRODUCTION

Since 2002, the bulk of Kelly's practice has included complex family law matters. Over the years and in two different states, Kelly Peterson earned a reputation for effectively handling high-conflict matters involving such areas as complex financial issues, substance abuse, child abuse/neglect (and false allegations thereof), mental health issues, and domestic violence. He has effectively represented his clients in literally thousands of court hearings.

Additionally, Kelly has helped resolve hundreds of cases in mediation, has represented abused and neglected children as a Guardian ad Litem, and represented clients in a variety of other civil areas.

After obtaining his law degree at BYU in 2000, Kelly clerked at the Utah Court of Appeals allowing him to develop appellate-quality research and writing ability. These skills later proved essential to quality representation of his clients.

In 2010, Kelly underwent the rigorous certification process to become a Child Welfare Law Specialist (CWLS). Few private attorneys in Utah hold this distinction, which is obtained through the National Association of Counsel for Children (NACC).

Because of his expertise in these areas, attorneys and therapists have invited Kelly to be a guest lecturer on areas such as: defending against dirty litigation tactics, forensic interviewing of adults, and the handling of expert witnesses in court. Also, Kelly compiled an extensive legal reference guide for family law and juvenile court that is used state-wide by family law attorneys, juvenile court attorneys, mediators and judges.

When not at the office, Kelly spends as much time as possible with his lovely wife and hilarious children.

How Is Parental Alienation Defined In Utah Law?

Parental alienation is not defined by Utah Law, though it is very common. It's something very fact sensitive. An attorney and a therapist that are experienced in this area are critical. There are different degrees of parental alienation. One lesser degree is disillusionment and parental alienation is not always related to divorce. It depends upon whether the parties were married or not.

Who Can Legally Determine If Parental Alienation Is Occurring?

Ultimately, it is the judge's decision whether parental alienation is occurring. They can rely on evidence presented to them by the parties and by third party professionals like therapists or custody evaluators. It seems many lawyers are afraid to get into a case involving parental alienation because it's so difficult to prove and it takes an enormous amount of work to do so.

What Is The Best Way To Deal With Parental Alienation Outside The Legal Realm?

Attorneys and therapists that are experienced in this area are the best bet for helping a situation involving parental alienation.

How Are Children Alienated From Either Parent In A Custody Dispute?

Causing alienation of a child against the other parent is a form of emotional abuse. There is no easy way to describe emotional abuse. The injuries are not physical and they don't leave physical scars. Individual acts of abuse can be excused as unintentional or atypical to the perpetrator. It is easy for the victim to experience a gradual desensitization to behaviors occurring in that context and then lose awareness that the norm has shifted. It is definitely harmful to a child.

Emotional abuse is the most common form of abuse yet the most difficult to demonstrate as a pattern. Like other forms of abuse, it exploits the child's dependency, innocence and selfhood. There is a famous attachment expert named John Bowlby who observed that pressure put on children to conform to parents' wishes can be crude or subtle but its effectiveness depends on the child's insistent desire to be loved and protected. Alienation, being a form of emotional abuse is no trick. Alienation can occur intentionally and with the full awareness of the parent or it can happen unintentionally.

It is important to note that alienation can occur by either parent. For purposes of discussion, Attorney Kelly Peterson discusses more about alienation by the other parent that can occur often unintentionally by profound lack of insight. He discusses various ways that alienation can occur and begins the conversation looking at the more unintentional kind because it is the most common form in his experience.

First, when dealing with an alienation case, one question that Attorney Peterson asks is, "Of all the people in this child's life, who has the most influence over that child?"

It's often the parent who the child is dependent on and usually that's the custodial parent. Often the alienated parent is the other parent. However, sometimes the roles are reversed and the custodial parent is alienated. One way this often happens is when parents divorce, and there is a parent who is very good at setting structure and boundaries, rules and chores into place. The other parent is more of a friend. Which one does the child gravitate to? Most likely it will be the one that he or she will have more fun with or the parent that doesn't enforce homework, chores, and other reasonable punishment. The child will often tend to gravitate towards or identify with that parent who is perhaps too indulgent.

Then what will happen sometimes is known as an exaggeration of differences where the parent that the child is gravitating toward and the child will attempt to exaggerate the differences between homes in an attempt to produce fear or anxiety in the child about going back to the other parent.

Things like, "I can't play the same things at mom's house as I can at dad's house."

Minor issues become a basis for exaggeration of differences in a child. Then, the alienating parent will often share personal details that exceed the child's cognitive and emotional abilities to handle. For example, when you look at loyalty conflict, children lack the emotional scaffolding to be able to handle conflict between their parents. A full grown mature adult can navigate between parental conflicts but a child doesn't have that emotional maturity. So what they tend to do is to reject the parent to simplify their lives. They have more black and white thinking than a mature adult would have.

They tend to go with the path of least resistance. Whichever parent will make his or her life easier, that's the parent he or she will side with. The thinking is, “I'm going to reject the other parent, not because I don't love them but because

I don't have the emotional maturity to be able to handle the conflict. I'm going to simplify my life."

As mentioned oftentimes that loyalty conflict is exacerbated when a parent shares personal details that exceed a child's cognitive and emotional abilities to handle. For example it could include things like who was the cause of the divorce, if there was an affair, if the other parent has a criminal history or other bad things the other parent is alleged to have done.

The child will be often reminded of the broken promises that the other parent has made or bad things that they have done that the child witnessed. Sometimes the alienating parent will misrepresent the rejected parent's feelings to a child to create hurt, resentment and psychological distance.

Another very common way for alienation to occur is allowing the child to practice rejection of the alienated parent without intervening and imposing consequences. Every parent would say that it is highly important to teach a child to be respectful and polite and obedient to adults but alienating parents create a bind and a lie for a child.

To further explain, it is trying to have a child apply that learning of being polite and respectful to adults and then kind of by their own actions teaching the child that it is only situational. This means, to teach the child that being nice and kind and all of those great things, is a value to be applied not always and not with all people; that it is ok to rude and disrespectful towards the alienated parent but not towards others. A parent would never put up with a child being disrespectful to a teacher or to a doctor. However, the alienating parent will often hide behind that child's choice disclaiming any responsibility for the relationship with the alienated parent and allow the child to be hateful without consequence. That is essentially passive support of the alienation.

Even if the alienated parent didn't cause the initial anger that the child has against the alienated parent, they can lend passive support to the process by allowing the child to continually practice rejection of the other parent. Other parents, the ones that do it more intentionally, will actually require devotion of the child and require rejection of the other parent. The ultimate sign of devotion to one parent becomes the renunciation of the other. In psychology that's often referred to as splitting. It is a common characteristic of adult personality disorders.

Going back to the bind and the lie, the bind is that you have to be respectful. The lie is that the alienating parent expects the child to learn the lesson of respect and to apply them appropriately when really he or she is okay with the child being disrespectful to the other parent. That creates a great deal of confusion and cognitive dissonance for the child. The effect of continual rejection on a child is that it has profound psychological implications or negative consequences both short term and long term for the rest of the child's life unless it's dealt with appropriately in therapy.

For example, if a child learns in their childhood to continually reject one of the two most important people in their life, what happens when they are 30 and their marriage is on the rocks? They have already established a pattern in their childhood of rejecting very important people. Now, what happens when they have a difficult child with special needs or a child that is obstinate? They have already practiced rejection of a very significant figure in their lives and it makes it easier to reject their own children. They can also contract other things like anxiety, depression and so on.

Research has demonstrated that children who have been enlisted into alienated procedures most often do so between the ages of 8 and 15. With age, there is a hardening of rejection that occurs because the children are able to maintain a consistent stance of anger and rigid refusal over a period of time. An alienating child can appear to be in charge and everyone is marching to their beat but the favored parent almost never insists that the child's drum beat change no matter how extreme. The alienating parent will play the favorite and allow the child to beat that drum without intervention.

It raises the question, if the child is left in the custody of the alienating parent, the child will only have one parent and if the custody is switched, the child will have two depending on the circumstances.

ALIENATING PARENTS WILL OFTEN HIDE BEHIND THE CHILD'S CHOICE

Alienating parents will often hide behind a child's feelings and choice. They say to themselves, "I can't change how he feels about you. I don't bad mouth you. I don't coach him to talk. I can't force him to talk to you. I have a rational discussion beforehand and then we let him choose what he wants to do."

Parents who do this haven't obviously thought the concept through thoroughly or if they have, they are intentionally alienating because a parent does play a role in a child's treatment of others. An alienating parent will fail to make the child answerable for any of the treatment that they meted out to the non-favored parent.

Teaching children to disrespect and demean the other parent, even when it occurs by not intervening corrupts the child's values and personality through the same learning process that has delivered reinforcement of our social values. A lot of times, one dynamic that occurs in the alienation is the when the child's real opportunities for sustaining a relationship with the non-favored parent becomes instead a platform or an opportunity for a child to list grievances, ultimatums and accusations against the non-favored parent. Sometimes these types of contacts are followed by long periods of isolation and no response. Hanging up when contact is attempted or requesting to change parenting time or to delay it.

The child's opportunity to have their perceptions corrected by actually spending time with the non-favored parent is delayed. This makes it harder to transition away from the corrupting environment maintained by the parent that is allowing all of this. One form of corruption is allowing the child to persist in a set of beliefs which supports the favored parent's posture against the non-favored parent. Favored parents who adopt a posture of passive support of the child's rejection of the other parent often attempt to convince themselves and others that they are not fully communicating anything to their child.

The child's posture and beliefs towards the non-favored parent tells the truth about the effect of the non-response of the passive parent. With every rejection of a call, every rejection of Skype time, of parent time or visitation, the child becomes more deeply entrenched in the alienating behavior.

Selective non correction and isolation from people who could give corrective experiences is another subtle way that alienation can occur. If an alienating parent is passive about a child's relationship with a non-favored parent, what that does is place exclusive responsibility on the child to maintain that relationship. The child is not allowed to be openly torn, so even if they secretly loved the other parent, they often won't express it.

Concerns Of Abuse From An Alienating Parent

Oftentimes the alienating parents will voice their concerns on how the child is being neglected with the other parent even though they don't really have significant evidence. They often only have suspicions.

Sometimes their abuse concerns are well met but not very insightful. However, they believe them so rigidly that their lack of evidence doesn't bother them. Alienating parents often want the courts or others to believe that their concerns for the child are centered around risks in the other parent's home but they can't demonstrate those risks. They want to rely on suspicions and innuendo instead. Parents who are alienating often fail to inform the other parent of significant events or failure to involve the non-favored parent in decision making.

Does Parental Alienation Constitute Violation Of A Custody Agreement?

Parental alienation can constitute a custody agreement, depending on what particular orders were stipulated in the agreement. If there are orders saying that neither party should disparage the other or allow others to do so, and that happens then that would constitute a violation of the stipulated orders and constitute contempt of court.

What Is Parental Alienation Syndrome?

A lot of times people get fixated on this diagnosis of parental alienation syndrome which has largely been debunked in literature. One of the reasons is that Parental Alienation Syndrome is not a forensic diagnostic tool. It often tends to focus on the motives of the alienating parent rather than their behavior. Unless somebody has a magic device that can actually determine someone's motives by getting into his or her head, it's not really useful to focus so much on the alienating parent's motives.

Instead of focusing on motives, they should be focused on the other parent's behavior. When Attorney Kelly Peterson tries a parental alienation case, he is less concerned with whether it's intentional or unintentional. He will often explain to the court that if it's intentional that's really bad.

If it's lack of insight then it's just as bad because then the parent is prone to continue their behavior because they lack the insight to foresee the impact of their behavior on the other parent. If they are doing it intentionally they are also likely to continue the behavior.

What Are Some Methods Of Proving Parental Alienation?

Proving parental alienation is difficult. It can be done, but oftentimes attorneys and parents will give up too soon. In Attorney Kelly Peterson's opinion and experience, one of the most powerful tools to help prove parental alienation is to depose the other party. For those that are unfamiliar, a deposition is an opportunity that an attorney has to question the other party, outside of the presence of the judge, for up to seven hours. There is a court reporter or a stenographer in attendance who puts the deponent, the person being deposed, under oath to tell the truth, the whole truth, and nothing but the truth. The deponent's attorney is there and can raise objections to any question that is asked, but the deponent still has to answer the question.

For example, if the attorney asks a question that opposing counsel determines or believes to be hearsay, he can state his objection, but the person being deposed has to answer the question regardless.

In deposing someone in an alienation case, here are some examples of how such a deposition might go and how it can be useful:

The first step for a deposition is to set the deponent up. The questioning attorney should ask the person if he or she has had their deposition taken before or testified at trial. The next step is to advise the deponent to answer all questions audibly and ask if he or she has any drugs, alcohol or memory conditions or impulse control problems that might negatively impact his or her testimony.

Next, Attorney Peterson sometimes asks the deponent about how to be honest. For example, he asks them if they understand what exaggeration is and how that's a form of deception. He asks if the person knows what minimization is and how that is a form of deception or how omitting important facts is a form of deception. Attorney Peterson gets the definition crystal clear from the very beginning that if someone is exaggerating, or is leaving important truths out, he or she is essentially lying.

Additionally Attorney Peterson introduces the concept of lack of insight at the beginning of a deposition. He asks if the individual has ever been deceptive through minimization, exaggeration, omitting important truths and those kinds of things. That sets the stage for when he catches the person in those types of behaviors later on.

Often Attorney Peterson will then go into parenting ability or co-parenting ability. He asks how they feel about the other parent and what do they think the other parent's strengths and weaknesses are. He also asks the deponent what he or she thinks his or her own strengths and weaknesses are and if he or she thinks there is anything wrong with either parent.

Attorney Peterson gets the deponent to explain all of the things about his or her parenting that he or she believes to be good or bad about the other side and he wants the person to commit to that. Once the person has committed himself or herself to those answers he then begins presenting more specific facts. He might ask if the deponent has ever engaged in a certain kind of behavior and he gets more and more specific in the questioning.

When deposing someone on parental alienation, the case has to be structured very carefully. One of the ways that Attorney Peterson begins is by asking about structure or boundaries. He is looking for what kind of structures or boundaries the alienating parent imposes on the child. Quite often that parent doesn't have any. They do not provide enough discipline for the child. They do not provide enough structure and boundaries. The reason that they do that is to gain the child's preference over the other parent.

Very often in alienation cases the alienated parent is actually the better parent. He or she ends up being the parent who institutes rules, structure, discipline and chores. The alienating parent often doesn't implement that kind of structure.

Attorney Peterson may ask questions like, "She doesn't really like rules, restrictions and chores. Does she?" or "This child is very attached to presents, isn't she? You love your daughter, right? You don't want to be overly harsh with her, do you?"

He also asks things like, "Are you on the side of being overly indulgent rather than being overly harsh? Do you think that you're too indulgent? Do you think you impose enough rules? What are the rules and restrictions in your household?"

In doing so, Attorney Peterson gets the person to commit themselves in those kinds of areas, he then begins going through the chronological specific events. He then starts asking things like, "What about this incident on this day?" or "Let's turn to exhibit seven. Do you see this record? Doesn't this show X, Y, or Z?"

All of a sudden the individual is now backpedaling from what they said earlier.

Another area that Attorney Peterson addresses during a deposition and that is he will ask the deponent whether they allow disrespect of other people including the other parent.

For example, “You would say that it’s pretty important to teach a child to be respectful and polite and obedient to adults, right? How do you teach the child to do that generally? List all the steps you do to teach the child to be respectful of others and yourself. Do you think you’re good at teaching the child to respect others?”

Attorney Peterson then will go through all of the incidents in which the other parent appears to have enabled the child to be disrespectful of others. He will then often go through how allowing or reinforcing practiced rejection of his client, or the alienating parent, affects the child.

“Do you think that the child’s been alienated, and what percentage of the blame do you think you bear?

“Who is responsible for the quality of the relationship between the child and the other parent?”

Often time parties will get tripped up on that question. What they don't realize is both parents have a responsibility to maintain a high quality of a relationship between the child and the other parent. However, alienating parents don't believe that. They think that the relationship between the other parent and the child is the other parent's business and not their own. When you expose that and ask the alienating parent whose job it is to help maintain the relationship very often the alienating parent will say it's the other parent's responsibility and that speaks volumes.

Additionally Attorney Peterson will sometimes then introduce concepts that perhaps the other parent has never thought about before such as research on alienation.

For example, one concept is that research demonstrates that children who have been enlisted into alienating postures most often do so between the ages of 8 and 15. Then, there is a hardening of the rejection because children are able to maintain a consistent stance of anger and rigid refusal over a long period of time.

Attorney Peterson will take the person through a lot of the psychological principles underpinning alienation and he will ask questions like, “Do you believe that that principle is true? Do you think that it applies in your case at all?”

A lot of times the individual has never thought about a particular concept like this before and now are being asked to consider the concept right there in the deposition. This requires the person to be really honest and often he or she doesn’t know what else to say.

Another area of parental alienation Attorney Peterson brings up during a deposition is passively allowing a child to persist in negative thoughts about the other parent as another form of alienating.

He asks how the alienating parent handles the situation when the child comes and complains about the target parent.

“Do you ever force the child to go?”

Often the answer is no. Instead they allow the child to persist in negative beliefs, and when the child makes a negative statement about the alienated parent, instead of trying to get the target parent’s perspective to find out what happened they immediately bite that hook line and sinker and begin validating and reinforcing that belief.

One quote from a psychologist is that alienated children can appear in charge when everyone is marching to their beat, but the favored parent almost never insists that the child's drum beating changes no matter how extreme. That's often the case where alienated children seem to be in charge, and an alienating parent passively allows it.

Attorney Peterson introduces these psychological principles and then asks the alienating parent if those principles ever apply to them.

"Have you ever done this? Has this ever happened in your case?"

Again, he gets the person to commit to the answers. After he or she has committed, he once again takes the chronology his client has done and go through it incident by incident by incident and reinforce that the other parent may have been passively allowing the child to persist in negative beliefs against the target parent.

Another thing that Attorney Peterson talks about during parental alienation cases is exaggerating differences between the parents and the children. For example, that could be claiming abuse or transferring anxiety to the child.

If a parent were to ask a child, "Does your other parent ever do A, B, or C when you are at his/her house? No?"

It's a way of really emphasizing the difference between the two parents to the detriment of the other parent and the child. So is talking about how abusive the other person is, or transferring anxiety.

Transferring anxiety may be where one parent exaggerates his or her emotions to a child and makes him or feel worry or sadness that the parent is in tears, for example. This could instill a fear for the child that there must be something to be worried about. Often personal details are shared that exceed the child's cognitive and emotional abilities to handle.

Attorney Peterson will go through those types of psychological principles as well, and then he will ask the alienating parent if he or she has ever done that. When they say no, he once again goes back to the chronology and shows incident by incident how they have done so.

Additionally Attorney Peterson will ask an alienating parent about abuse concerns. He will get them to talk of how abusive or how horrible the other parent, his client, is and then he will go through the actual evidence, or rather, lack of evidence that they have to demonstrate this. When going through all of the evidence, there is often a pattern of exaggerated or distorted beliefs of how dangerous the target parent really is. However, again the idea is to first get the parent to commit to it.

Oftentimes the source of their information is unreliable hearsay statements from the child. If the child is truthful that is one thing. However, oftentimes a child is triangulating both parents, telling each what they want to hear. There are all kinds of reasons why a child might triangulate, including if they feel pressure to report what the questioning parent wants to hear, or because they genuinely prefer the alienating parent because of that parent's lack of structure or rules and boundaries.

Attorney Peterson also asks the alienating parent to define every single reason why he or she believes the other parent is not fit and he gets them to commit to it. Next, if the child is not credible, he will get the parent to commit that he or she is basing a lot of his or her testimony on the child's statements. He will go through and start talking about any evidence that he has of the child's lack of credibility; if the child has made contradictory statements in the past or has said things just to get their way.

He might ask the alienating parent, "How credible do you think this child is? What about this statement or that statement? This is the information you're relying on and concluding that my client is abusive."

Additionally over involving a child in decision making and then hiding behind the child's choice is one of the biggest ways that parents alienate. In these situations Attorney Peterson asks questions about how important the child is in the decision process. Often alienating parents will say the child is very important in the process. However, at trial he or she will be made to understand, often by expert witnesses in the court, the child is too immature to make a reasonable decision most of the time. Hiding behind an immature child's choice and relinquishing the role of the parent is not helpful to the child.

Additionally Attorney Peterson will ask the parent what he or she thinks the long term consequences would be for the child when practicing rejection of the primary attachment figure of a parent. He may ask, "If a child practices rejection of a parent over and over again what impact will that have on them later in life when they have a rough time with a spouse or if they have an autistic child that's difficult? Won't that increase the likelihood that they will reject spouse or children?"

By hiding behind the child's choice the parent is often helping the child practice rejection, which is going to serve them poorly in the future. Once again, when these things come up, Attorney Peterson will go back to the chronology of all of the times that the parent has hidden behind the child's choice. He then starts to discuss with the deponent all of the various things that the parent could have done but failed to do, such as consequences for the child who is practicing rejection against the other parent, like refusing to see him or her.

Another area of important to look at in a deposition is interference with parent time and failure to adequately support the parent time, which are other methods by which alienation can occur. These can be more subtle than outright disparaging the other parent. There are multiple and varied methods by which alienation can occur. If someone has an attorney who understands them and who knows which psychologists or therapists can help identify what's really going on, then that person has a much better chance of demonstrating that alienation is occurring.

Oftentimes alienating parents will blame negative behavior of the child on the other parent, or the target parent. To address these issues, Attorney Peterson will ask questions such as, "Well you love your child and she has some behavioral problems, yes? Do you believe there's any increase or decrease in behavioral problems after a visit with the target parent?"

They inevitably will say yes, that there is an increase in these bad behaviors. So Attorney Peterson will then go through the research and quote the research showing how the alienating parents seem to seize multiple opportunities to link the child's negative behavior to association with the other parent.

Attorney Kelly Peterson will go through all of the ways in the chronology to show the alienating parent has done exactly that and blamed negative behavior on the child. He will then ask questions about how the parent may have recruited others to their agenda; another therapist for example.

Once the deponent has been nailed down on their actual attitudes and beliefs in a deposition, that deposition transcript will be used to demonstrate to a custody evaluator and to the court, exactly the ways that the alienating parent is behaving in a way that would tend to diminish the love and affection of the child towards the target parent.

After a deposition, if the person deviates from his or her previous answers, Attorney Kelly Peterson can then use their deposition transcript, making it very clear to the court what's really going on.

KEEPING A JOURNAL OF INCIDENTS WITH THE ALIENATING PARENT

Attorney Kelly Peterson advises all of his clients to keep a journal of any incidents that occur in custody cases. For parental alienation cases, he has them go a step further.

One of the things that he does to help reduce their costs, while at the same time increasing the efficiency of their attorney, is he has clients do a chronology of events with very specific instructions. The chronology is designed to weed out the irrelevant information from the relevant.

The goal of the chronology is to spoon feed the evidence as clearly and simply to the fact finder, backing up every assertion with citations to supporting documentation. Judges are people too, and their eyes glaze over if there's too much "he said, she said" disorganized, gray areas or irrelevant information shoved at them.

Too many people make the mistake of just dumping a bunch of that type of information on a judge and expecting them to magically sort it out. Judges do not have super-human abilities of concentration, patience, or avoidance. The attorney's job is to reduce and simplify making it easy for the judge to clearly see the important information.

Also by doing this, it reduces the amount of time that the attorney has to spend sorting through all of the documents and learning all of the facts, thereby significantly reducing the amount of money clients spend on attorney's fees.

Attorney Peterson has his clients make two columns. On the left they put the approximate date or the date range in which the event took place. On the right, they are to describe the event in full sentences. Often people write their feelings in the journal. They write characterizations or conclusionary statements when they should only be recording only facts.

For example, someone may write, "He was belligerent and abusive towards me."

Whether something was belligerent or abusive is a conclusion or a characterization of a fact, not a fact. The court is the one who decides if a behavior rises to the level of belligerent or abusive. Clients should only assert facts. For instance, "He pushed me and yelled."

That is a fact, not a conclusion. There is a difference. On the left-hand side, Attorney Peterson doesn't have them explain the relevance of the fact that is on the right-hand side. Usually, the relevance of the fact will be apparent without further explanation, but there are exceptions.

If they feel that further explanation is necessary Attorney Peterson will have them do so in a footnote. It's always better to have clients lean on the side of too much information instead of too little. If they think something could be relevant but they aren't sure, it is best to add it in. It's easier to remove an irrelevant detail than have to go back and get additional details later on. However, generally the person should go back in chronology all the way to the beginning of the relationship with the other side.

Some people start by memory. Others want to collect all relevant documents including emails, affidavits, court orders, text messages, transcripts, police reports and whatever documentation supports their position. Attorney Peterson then has the client put everything in chronological order and then start highlighting. Anything that is highlighted then gets used to start building the beginning of the chronology. Once that information is put together, it will create a kind of scaffolding or a framework that can be built upon from the things that only come by memory and there is no documentation backing it up. Attorney Peterson encourages his clients when they are doing this to use actual quotes from text messages, emails, reports, orders and what was said.

Additionally he advises to do the same even if it is only by memory and there are no documents to back it up. Quote everyone from the opposing party. Quote the children, the therapist, case workers, police officers, doctors, etc., even if it is hearsay.

Attorney Peterson also has his clients go ahead and write the things that are detrimental to their case; things that they don't necessarily want the judge to know about. The reason behind this is because he, as the attorney, needs to be aware of any possible issues that could come up. He has them do that in red text so he knows what to consider removing or tweaking before the chronology or the facts in the chronology are released to anyone.

As they are doing this chronology, if a fact can only be supported by a memory that's okay. However, if the fact can also be supported by documentation such as a text message, an email, or a therapy record, for example, Attorney Peterson will have the client assign it to an exhibit number, and then cite to the exhibit immediately after writing the fact. When they go through this process it lays out their entire case beautifully beyond what a normal journal entry would be. It significantly reduces their attorney fees while at the same time making the attorney more efficient in their case.

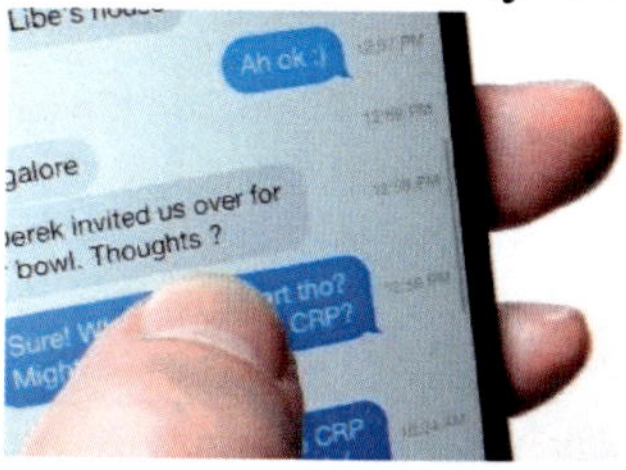

Is It Okay To Talk To The Child About The Alienating Parent's Behavior?

If the child spontaneously brings up the alienating parent's behavior or spontaneously starts talking, one of the things that Attorney Kelly Peterson has his clients do is record the conversation if possible. The parent should not, however, be pumping the child for additional information. If the child is talking about it spontaneously, however, he or she shouldn't be told not to talk about it. It may be ok to ask vague questions but the person should not be forensically interviewing the child. That's inappropriate.

As the parent, you can comfort the child but not in a way that disparages the other side, or in a way that pumps the child inappropriately for more information. That would be tainting the child's credibility as well as the parent's own credibility.

Should A Conversation With The Child Be Recorded In The Journal Of Events?

In the state of Utah it is legal for one party to record a conversation so long as they're a part of it, whether it is in person or over the phone. If obtained appropriately, some of the most compelling evidence one can have is the child talking about what is going on. It's just that it has to be spontaneous and it can't be engineered. The child can't be pumped for additional information. It has to be somewhat spontaneous on the child's part, and any follow-up questions from the parent have to be very vague and non-leading. If they ask a leading question, then that automatically diminishes the child's credibility.

How Can Other Adults Be Utilized In Parental Alienation Cases?

Other people can be used as witnesses in parental alienation cases, such as what they have observed the alienating parent say or do in front of the child. Those observations and statements are important.

One of the things that Attorney Kelly Peterson has his clients do is search for such witnesses. If there are people that his client is aware of who has observed alienating kinds of behavior from an alienating parent, then their statements and their testimony become significant. Keep in mind there can be passive and active alienation. Just because a witness doesn't observe something overt and intentional as far as alienation goes, that doesn't mean they are not observing alienation.

Causation Of A Child's Misbehavior

If a child is misbehaving in the alienating parent's home, they will blame the non-favored parent for the child's misbehavior. They will link the child's misbehavior to association with the alienated parent. Some scholars say that doing that is not a deliberate strategy but a part of the favored parent's core beliefs about the other parent and their desires to be rid of the other parent out of their own lives. It becomes a primitive psychological defense of a fragile sense of self in the favored parent. They often will decline to take any responsibility for the child's misbehavior and content themselves with just blaming the other person.

Another common strategy used by alienating parents is to recruit others to their cause. Oftentimes these are therapists or doctors or DCFS. As far as therapists or doctors, professionals are very often uninformed and unaware of the history of the case and are consequently easily misled by the alienating parents. Mental health professionals are often inadequately trained concerning divorce and the standards of practice are associated with court involved therapy, particularly if they are unaware of the Alliance of Family and Conciliation Courts guidelines for court involved therapy.

Oftentimes if they are unfamiliar with those guidelines or similar principles, competent counselors can find themselves in challenging circumstances where they veer from the areas that they are solemnly trained and experienced in. They and don't have the background necessary to anticipate and guard against the manipulations of an alienation case. More therapists should have the role or the responsibility of making recommendations for changes of parenting time or changes of custody to a court if they are a treating therapist.

If they are a forensic therapist that is specifically tasked with a forensic evaluation, then that is different but if they are actually treating a child or a parent, that's not their role. Sometimes therapists that mean well will fail to include the other parent in knowing the extent that it's appropriate to do so. It's a mighty thin pancake that doesn't have two sides. So that therapist never gets the other side of the allegations. Oftentimes there is pressure on the child to report bad experiences with the alienated parent. A lot of times that happens unintentionally and well-meaningly from the alienating parent.

For example, if a child comes home from visitation and mom is on the phone, the child isn't getting the attention he wants and he says something bad happened at the father's house. What does mom do? She instantly hangs up the phone and gives the child all her attention. All of a sudden, the child now has an emotional pat on the head for making a disclosure that something bad happened at dad's house. He is going to remember that and now he knows that is the way to get attention from mom and that's talking negatively about dad. That heightens the vigilance of mom and then she is constantly on the alert for that kind of thing.

That's just one subtle way and there are all kinds of ways that parents pressure children unintentionally into making disclosures, however exaggerative, against the other parent.

Strategies To Avoid Negative Interaction With Alienating Parent

First, Attorney Kelly Peterson instructs his clients not to engage in arguments in person or over the phone; to remain civil. Name calling is never acceptable and the individual should avoid accusations. It is okay for a parent to state his or her position on a matter respectfully. However, it is not okay to become abusive in language, be accusatory, and spiteful. If someone does that, it will come back to bite them. If the other parent is doing that kind of thing often Attorney Peterson has clients record it and then hold up that mirror to the court and ask for orders to prevent that kind of conduct.

Another common way of avoiding conflict with the alienating parents is by limiting the communication to text or email. Keep communication to child-related issues only so that there can't be accusations about why a marriage failed or something to that effect.

Sometimes the court will order all communication to be civil and sometimes that will do the trick. Other times more draconian methods are called for. For example, there are times where the conflict between two parties is so extreme that they find new and creative ways to be uncivil with each other while attempting to present the image of civility. Additionally it could be a case where it is not so much the content as the frequency and timing of the communication that becomes harassing to the other side.

In cases such as this often professional communications services can be used, where the parties are only able to communicate via email. That email is screened by a third party professional who, if they read the email and they conclude that it's too accusatory or too negative, they send it back to be rewritten before passing it on to the recipient. They have specific communication guidelines. In the state of Utah one of the most effective third party communication agencies is an agency called The Family Academy, otherwise known as ACAFS, whose phone number is 801-377-5050.

At What Point Should Someone Seek Court Orders Restricting An Alienating Parent?

When it comes to someone seeking a court order restricting the alienating parent, Attorney Kelly Peterson advises, if something negative has happened only once and it doesn't really bother anyone, then don't worry about it. However, if the situation or an incident is negatively impacting the non-alienating parent and his or her relationship with the child, negatively impacting the child, at that point they should seek court orders restraining that kind of conduct.

Upon Suspicion Of Parental Alienation Can Someone Ignore Visitation Orders?

The court is generally going to make the assumption that parent time with both parents is in the children's best interest. If a parent unilaterally decides that is not the case without going through the proper court procedures to limit the other parent's parent time, then he or she is engaging in what's called "self-help." This is where he or she is intentionally limiting the relationship between a parent and a child without the approval of the court.

If a relationship with or behaviors from the other parent are causing harm to the child then it needs to be handled through the proper procedures of demonstrating that to the court. Then the non-alienating parent can ask for relief such as limiting parent time or supervision or therapeutic supervised parent time, a parental fitness evaluation, etc.

However, unless the individual is able to demonstrate the evidence supporting his or her position, limiting the child's contact unilaterally with the other parent is going to backfire. The court will likely believe that the parent who has limited the contact with the abusive parent is really the offender.

Is Having A Child Psychologically Evaluated Feasible In A Parental Alienation Case?

More often than not having a child psychologically evaluated is beneficial in a parental alienation case. However, it is important to be careful about the type of psychologist that is used. It is best practice to use someone who is familiar with and has experience in being a court involved therapist; somebody who understands how therapy is impacted by court involvement.

Often when people go in to see a therapist they really want help. They are candid and honest with the therapist. Litigation often changes all of that. Oftentimes one litigant will want to use the therapist as a super charge to their argument. Therefore, they will present this distorted information to the therapist in hopes that he or she will rely on that information to render an opinion about what is in the child's best interest. It's absolutely inappropriate for a therapist to do so. However, many if not most therapists don't understand how litigation changes their own ethical rules.

There is an organization called The Association of Family and Conciliation Courts. This is an association consisting of attorneys and therapists that has promulgated additional guidelines to help keep therapists out of hot water when there is court involvement. A therapist has to approach a court-involved case much differently than any other types of client.

Here are some of the AFCC guidelines that should be adhered to and that therapists are often not even aware of: The court-involved therapist should not render opinions in psycho-legal issues such as parental capacity, child custody, validity of an abuse allegation, joint or sole custody, as these are beyond the scope of the treatment role and properly the providence of other professionals in the court.

The court-involved therapist should also avoid service simultaneously in multiple roles, particularly if these multiple roles create a conflict of interest.

A court-involved therapist should not serve simultaneously as a therapist and an evaluator or as a therapist and a friend. Similarly, a court-involved therapist is strongly discouraged from performing different roles sequentially.

For example, a therapist who becomes an evaluator has to understand that the difference between a therapist and an evaluator are very different. They might have the same licensure, but the roles are very dissimilar. In order to become a therapist, you have to develop a therapeutic alliance and actually treat someone. In order to be an evaluator your job is to find facts. That means an evaluator needs to be dispassionate, remain objective, should not form an alliance, but instead use the instruments of the trade to help determine what the facts are and then render an opinion to the court. That is the difference between therapeutic work and forensic work.

Therapists often will write letters to the court saying, "I've been treating this child for so long and in my opinion it's in the best interest of the child that they stay with their mother."

That is engaging in both therapeutic work and forensic work simultaneously and is unethical. The treating therapist cannot give recommendations to the court including statements regarding what is in the child's best interest if they are providing therapy. The child's "best interests" is the province of the court or the forensic expert witness. A court-involved therapist should not allow their role to be misused.

The court-involved therapist should also use particular caution to ensure that he or she has accurate data on which to base any opinions or assessments. The responsibility is to form and express such opinions within the confines of the therapeutic role and available information while remaining cognizant of the impact of court involvement on the family and on treatment information. There are many other such guidelines that if a therapist is unaware they could end up doing more harm than good.

WHAT IS A GUARDIAN AD LITEM IN UTAH?

Guardian ad Litem in the state of Utah is a court appointed attorney who represents the child; both the child's wishes and the child's best interests. If there is a conflict between the child's wishes and what the guardian ad litem believes to be the child's best interests, then the guardian ad litem has to represent both and say something like "Your Honor, Here are my client's desires and here's why he thinks it. Here's what I think is in my client's best interest and here's why I think that best for the child."

The court is going to assume that the guardian ad litem's arguments to the court are in the child's best interest and what the child wishes, or at least is not contrary to the child's wishes, unless the guardian ad litem specifically states otherwise.

Is It A Good Idea To Ask The Court For A Guardian Ad Litem If Parental Alienation Is Suspected?

Whether or not to ask the court for a guardian ad litem ("GAL"), depends on a variety of things. In the state of Utah in district court where divorce and custody actions take place public guardian ad litems were done away with in 2013. The public office of guardian ad litem are court appointed attorneys that represent the child. They are exclusively appointed in juvenile court where there are allegations of abuse or neglect, often with DCFS involvement or the attorney general involvement. This is where protective supervision services are implemented by the court or a child is removed at least temporarily from a parent. However, in district court where custody actions take place, a private guardian ad litem can be appointed and very often the court will require the parents to pay for it.

Once a private guardian ad litem is appointed it is unknown who will selected unless the parties stipulate to a particular individual. If the parties know that a particular attorney is on the private guardian ad litem roster they can stipulate to that person. However, if they do not agree then it's the luck of the draw. The person might or might not have good training about litigation, about how to interview children, about child development, about child-related issues, etcetera. Therefore it is a risk to request a random "GAL." The other thing is that the court will very often require one or both parties to pay the attorney's fees of the guardian ad litem.

This can be very expensive to pay both the parent's own attorney's fees plus half the guardian ad litem's fees. To boil it down, it can be risky to do so and it should be done carefully on a case by case basis.

Can Any False Allegations Made By The Alienating Parent Be Retracted In Court?

Certain things can be stricken from the record for various reasons. However, that's more rare than common. It is more common at trial if somebody says something that lacks foundation or is hearsay. At trial an attorney can object and move to strike. If the court grants the objection and the motion to strike, then it is stricken from the record and it cannot be used for any purpose. However, if somebody puts it in an affidavit and files it with a motion early on in the case, a motion to strike anything that is hearsay or without foundation that was not personally observed etc. can be filed. An attorney has to stay on top of that.

The most frequently that I see false or distorted information being presented is before trial. It's at affidavit or temporary orders hearings where people are just filing things left and right or proffering testimony. But you don't have the opportunity to actually examine or cross-examine them on the stand until much later on the proceedings. The best way to counter that is in the moment, right when it happens. If somebody files an affidavit that has false or distorted information, then you file your objection to that immediately.

Temporary orders hearings are often done by proffer, meaning that instead of evidence being taken, instead of a witness being put on the stand subject to examination and cross-examination, an attorney will stand up and say, "Your honor, here is my client. If he were called to testify today he would say what he said in his affidavit that has been filed before the court."

An attorney needs to object to that and move to strike immediately at the pre-trial proceedings. That said, those things are not going to be terribly binding at trial.

How Do You Correct That False Or Distorted Information With The Child?

If a parent is disparaging the other parent or is reinforcing a negative view of the other parent to the child, typically that is handled in family therapy. You can get that court ordered to where the parties or parent and the child are ordered to be in therapy to help address things like that.

DISCLAIMER

This publication is intended to be informational only. No legal advice is being given, and no attorney-client relationship is intended to be created by reading this material. If you are facing legal issues, whether criminal or civil, seek professional legal counsel to get your questions answered.

Law Office of Kelly Peterson
2696 N University Ave.,
Suite 240 Provo, UT 84604
(801) 375-0484
www.kmpetersonlaw.net

Made in the USA
Middletown, DE
06 August 2025

11832167R00033